DOCUMENTING DISABILITY

Strategies for Medical Providers

Law Offices of Lisa Douglas
2300 Main Street
North Little Rock, AR 72114
501-798-0004

739 South 7th Street
Suite 2
Heber Springs, AR 72543

www.LisaGDouglas.com

DISCLAIMER

This Book is Not Legal Advice

This information is general in nature and should not be relied on as a substitute for legal advice.

This book is provided as an education service by Law Offices of Lisa Douglas.

TABLE OF CONTENTS

Foreward v

Why this book 1

Familiarity With Social Security Administration's (SSA's) Language and Criteria 2

Five Questions SSA Considers in Determining Disability 2

Role of Medical Providers 4

Social Security Disability Insurance (SSDI) 5

The Social Security Administration's Definition of Disability 6

Disability Defined 7

The Five Step Evaluation Process Used to Determine Disability for Adults 8

      Step 1: Is the claimant engaging in substantial activity? 8
      Step 2: Does the applicant have a severe impairment? 8
      Step 3: Does the applicant suffer from an impairment? 9
      Step 4: Does the applicant have the residual functional capacity to per-
             form past relevant work? 10
      Step 5: Does the applicant have the residual functional capacity to per-
             form any other work? 10

Using the Social Security Administration's Listing of Impairments 12

SSA's Description of The Listing Of Impairments 13

Medical Considerations; 20 C.F.R. § 416.925 Listing of Impairments in appendix
      1 of subpart P of part 404 13

Who Can Document a Medical Impairment? 15

APPENDICES
      A   20 C.F.R. § 404.1526, Medical Equivalence 16

B   SSR 96-8p: Policy Interpretation Ruling Titles Ii and Xvi: Assessing Residual Functional Capacity in Initial Claims 18

C   20 C.F.R. § 404.1513, Medical and Other Evidence of Your Impairment(s) 31

D   20 C.F.R. § 416.913, Medical and Other Evidence of Your Impairments 34

E   Code of Federal Regulations 20 Appendix 2 to Subpart P of Part 404 — Medical Vocational Guidelines 37

200.00 Introduction. 37

201.00 Maximum sustained work capability limited to sedentary work as a result of severe medically determinable impairment(s). 40

202.00 Maximum sustained work capability limited to light work as a result of severe medically determinable impairment(s). 43

203.00 Maximum sustained work capability limited to medium work as a result of severe medically determinable impairment(s). 45

FOREWORD

In evaluating disability claims, this 5 step evaluation process is used by the Social Security Administration (SSA):

1.   Is the applicant no longer able to work 8 hours a day, 5 days a week, due to disability?

2.   Does the applicant have severe impairment?

3.   Does the applicant suffer from an impairment which meets or equals the severity of a listing?

4.   Can the applicant do any of his/her past relevant work?

5.   Can the applicant do other work that exists in the national economy, given his/her residual functional capacity, age, education, and work experience?

WHY THIS BOOK?

This book was written to inform clinicians about documentation of the medical impairments to support their patient's application for disability benefits. Educating clinicians regarding documentation of relevant facts is the first step in improving an applicants success. The medical records are the heart of the applicants case. Without the adequate documentation, the applicant's claim will likely fail.

Diagnostic tests provided by clinicians are considered at steps 2, 3, 4 and 5 of the evaluation process. At step 3 of the evaluation process, documentation of certain medical conditions can automatically qualify a claimant for disability. The criteria for establishing these conditions can be found in the Social Security Administration's listing of Impairments.

Clinicians who understand this evaluation process and who use the Listing of Impairments and document accordingly can provide the medical documentation necessary to support a disability claim.

It is not uncommon for a disability claim to initially be denied. Research shows that over 75% of those who initially apply for benefits are denied. However, research also shows that more than 75% of persons who appeal their cases and have representation are later approved for benefits.

This book was written to help guide the clinician through the documentation process to improve the success of applicants. In many cases it will take approximately two years before an applicant's claim is actually decided. But with proper documentation on the front end, the wait could be reduced.

This book is too limited to explore every issue or address each possible question you may have.

Further, this book is not intended to give legal advice and nothing in this book is legal advice. Obtaining this book from me does not create an attorney-client relationship between us.

Familiarity With Social Security Administration's (SSA's) Language and Criteria

Clinicians who provide medical evaluations or reports for Social Security Disability applicants, should become familiar with SSA's listing of impairments and the language used therein. Disability assessments are more easily evaluated and more focused when the clinicians are acquainted with SSA's language and criteria used by the disability examiners.

The medical evaluations and reports should include the applicable listings and numbers from the SSA's listing of impairments. Further, this documentation should address the criteria for each impairment. This practice will make the disability assessments focused and therefore, should result in fewer denials.

The best way to document a disability is to identify a medical Listing, furnish medical evidence of the impairment, and document functional limitations that have resulted from it. If the applicant meets the criteria for one or more of the Listings, the determination of disability will be relatively easy.

Five Questions SSA Considers in Determining Disability

The Social Security Administration has developed a five step test to determine if a disability exists according to their definition. When a claim is initially filed, it will go through this five step evaluation process.

The five questions to consider in determining whether or not a person is disabled according to the strict definition as set out by the Social Security Administration are as follows:

1.   Is the applicant gainfully employed? Gainfully employed means the applicant makes more than $940.00 per month or more.

2.   Is the applicant's condition severe? (The condition can be mental or physical or both, either way it interferes with basic activities at work.)

3.   Is the applicant's condition found in their list of disabling conditions?

(You can find these online through the SSA website.[1]

    4.   Can the applicant do the work he/she previously did?

    5.   Can the applicant do any other type of work?

In brief, the aforementioned five factors are a checklist to determine potential eligibility for Social Security Disability benefits. If the claimant is not working, then proceed to step two to determine if their condition interferes with work related activities. If it does not then they are not considered disabled. So, overall, they must pass the first two criteria before their claim will be considered.

If they are not gainfully employed and their condition does interfere with work then proceed to step three. Under step three if their condition is found in SSA's list of medical conditions then they are automatically deemed disabled. If their condition is not found on SSA's list of medical conditions then proceed to step four.

Here at step four, the clinician must determine if the claimant's medical condition interferes with their ability to perform the work they previously did. If it does then proceed to step five. If they cannot perform their previous job, is there any other job they can perform? Here SSA considers their age, education, work experience, and any skills they may have. If they cannot adjust to other work, their claim will be approved. However, if they can adjust to other work, their claim will be denied. This five step test will be addressed in more detail throughout this book.

Overall there are two ways to be found disabled under this Social Security Administration checklist: (1) A finding that the claimant's impairment meets an impairment described in the SSA's listing of impairments; or (2) A combination of the medical and vocational issues qualifies the claimant for disability.

---

[1] www.socialsecurity.gov/disability/professionals/bluebook/AdultListings.htm.

Role of Medical Providers

Medical evidence of the claimant's condition that results in disability is required to establish a claim for SSDI. The claimant relies on the clinician to provide the medical documentation they need in order to support their claim. Through a clear understanding of the process, a clinician can improve the chances of success for the initial applicant by providing the documentation as set out in the Disability Evaluation guidelines (Blue Book), found online.[2]

SSA regulations place special emphasis on evidence from the primary care physician because they are likely to be the ones most able to provide a detailed longitudinal picture of the claimant's impairments. The thought is the treatment received from the primary care physician will provide a more comprehensive report due to the ongoing treatments rather than a one time hospitalization or a brief consultative examination. Therefore, timely, accurate, and sufficient medical documentation from treating sources expedite the processing of the claim because they can greatly reduce or eliminate the necessity for additional medical evidence to complete the claim. SSA, *Consultative Examination Guide.*[3]

Merely confirming a medical diagnosis is insufficient to document a disability. The role of the clinician is to provide documentation and evidence of the disability. Medical professionals are asked to provide the facts, i.e. diagnostic tests, diagnoses with signs and symptoms such as functional limitations. These are the things that are necessary to determine disability. That is why a mere statement that the patient is disabled is insufficient for the SSA.

In summary, documentation of medical conditions that meet the SSA's criteria and documentation of functional impairments that result from the disabling health conditions, assessed over a period of time, are essential elements that are required to establish the claimant's disability claim.

---

[2] www.socialsecurity.gov/disability/professionals/bluebook.

[3] www.ssa.gov/disability/professionals/greenbook/ce-evidence.htm.

Social Security Disability Insurance (SSDI)

Successful applicants for social security disability insurance must have a recent work history. Unlike Social Security Income, SSDI is not contingent upon the income or assets of the applicant.

To qualify for SSDI, the applicant must be disabled pursuant to the Social Security Disability guidelines and must have worked a specific number of quarters out of the past 40 calendar quarters. The SSDI benefit amount is calculated on the applicants work history. However, applicants who do not qualify for SSDI, may qualify for Social Security Income.

SSDI beneficiaries are eligible for Medicare coverage after they have received SSDI benefits for 24 months.

The Social Security Administration's Definition of Disability

In order to qualify for Social Security Disability benefits, the applicant must be determined disabled according to the following Federal definition:

A disabled adult is defined as someone who is 18 years of age or older and is: "... unable to engage in any substantial gainful activity by reason of any medically determinable physical or mental impairment which can be expected to result in death or which has lasted or can be expected to last for a continuous period of not less than 12 months...." (42 U.S.C. § 1382c(a)(3) (A); 42 U.S.C. § 423(d)(1)(A))

To satisfy the Federal definition of disability, claimants must have sufficient medical documentation of an impairment, be it physical or mental. The medical documentation should include the signs and symptoms of the disability complained of along with laboratory and diagnostic tests to substantiate the disability claim.

Disability Defined

To qualify for social security disability, you must meet a strict criteria. Part of Social Security's definition of disability is the inability to work any job. That means that if you are a roofer and can no longer perform this strenuous job due to back problems, but you can sit and perform a less strenuous job like assembling watches on an assembly line, then you are not disabled under Social Security Administration's guidelines. Even working part time shows that you have the ability to work.

In addition the disability must be expected to last for twelve continuous months or be expected to end in death.

Further the condition must be a "medically determinable impairment." You cannot be determined to be disabled just because you say you are disabled. You have to have medical documentation to prove your disability. The doctor must back up his/her medical diagnosis of the impairment with medical history, diagnostic tests and laboratory results.

To summarize, in order to be found disabled for purposes of the social security administration your condition must be:

1.   A medically determinable impairment.

2.   Functionally limiting so that all work is precluded.

3.   Expected to last for twelve continuous months or be expected to end in death. A statement from the treating clinician regarding the anticipated duration of the disability is helpful to qualify the claimant's application for disability benefits.

The Five Step Evaluation Process Used to
Determine Disability for Adults

Step 1: Is the claimant engaging in substantial activity?

Substantial gainful activity (SGA) is the performance of a task that is resulting in income that equals or exceeds an amount set by the Social Security Administration.

The fact that a claimant can do some work, means that he/she is not disabled for the purposes of the Social Security Definition of disability.

Step 2: Does the applicant have a severe impairment?

If the claimant passed step one, then at step two is the threshold of inquiry regarding the severity of the claimant's impairment. This step is used to weed out weak claims. Here the evidence; i.e., medical documentation, lab results, diagnostic tests; are examined to determine if the claimant meets this threshold test. It is also here that a medical provider's detailed documentation can assist the claimant in his/her quest for disability benefits. Documentation as to the severity, intensity, and persistence of the disability are crucial at this step.

Symptoms, such as pain, fatigue, shortness of breath, weakness, or nervousness, will not be found to affect an individual's ability to do basic work activities unless the individual first establishes by objective medical evidence (i.e., signs and laboratory findings) that he or she has a medically determinable physical or mental impairment(s) and that the impairment(s) could reasonably be expected to produce the alleged symptom(s). *See* 2. SSR 96-4p Titles II and XVI: Symptoms, Medically Determinable Physical and Mental Impairments, and Exertional and Nonexertional Limitations. The finding that an individual's impairment(s) could reasonably be expected to produce the alleged symptom(s) does not involve a determination as to the intensity, persistence, or functionally limiting effects of the symptom(s). However, once the requisite relationship between the medically determinable impairment(s) and the alleged symptom(s) is established, the intensity, persistence, and limiting effects of the symptom(s) must be considered along with the objective medical and other evidence in determining whether the impairment or combination of impairments is severe.[4]

---

[4] http://www.ssa.gov/OP_Home/rulings/di/01/SSR96-03-di-01.html.

An impairment is considered severe if it interferes with the individual's ability to perform basic activities such as: walking, standing, lifting, sitting, pushing, pulling, concentration, lifting, carrying, memory, ability to follow simple instructions, hearing, speaking, etc. A severe impairment is the minimal level impairment necessary to meet SSA's definition of disability. If the impairment is not considered severe by SSA, then the claim for disability is denied. If the impairment is considered severe, then proceed to step three.

Step 3: **Does the applicant suffer from an impairment** that meets or equals the Listing Of Impairments?

The Listing of Impairments is published by the SSA. It contains prescribed physical or mental conditions that are considered so severe, that being diagnosed with these automatically deems the person disabled according to SSA.

The Listing of Impairments at is available in print and online.[5] The publication is entitled *Disability Evaluation under Social Security* and is known as the Blue Book. Here the SSA lists each system of the human body along with the criteria that must be met for each disabling condition. There are two different listings, one for adult and one for child. For the purposes of this book the focus is on adults. Or you can order a hard copy of this book free of charge from the Social Security Administration's Office of Supply and Warehouse Management, 239 Supply Building, 6301 Security Blvd., Baltimore, MD 21235.

If the available medical documentation shows the claimant has a disability that is identified in the Listing Of Impairments and it is expected to last for twelve months or more then the claimant will be determined to be disabled according to SSA's definition and should be awarded disability benefits.

However, many times claimants are frequently denied disability benefits even though they have a disability that is found within the Listing Of Impairments, simply because the medical documentation is lacking. In other words, the medical documentation does not support all the required elements of the relevant listing and/or the duration of the disability is not specified. Therefore, knowledge of the elements as required by the listing and documenting accordingly are critical for the success of a claimant.

---

[5] www.socialsecurity.gov/disability/professionals/bluebook.

A person may also qualify for benefits at this step, despite the fact their impairments do not meet a Listing as identified in the SSA's Listing of Impairments. The claimant can meet the disability standard by possessing impairments that are intrinsically similar to a Listing if the medical findings are at least equal in severity and duration to the listed findings (20 C.F.R. 404.1526) See What is Medical Equivalence under Appendix A

Step 4: Does the applicant have the residual functional capacity to perform past relevant work?

If the clinician is unable to establish a disability pursuant to the SSA's listed impairments or an equivalent condition, then the applicant's Residual Functional Capacity must be evaluated.

Residual Functional Capacity (RFC) is the maximum amount of activities the claimant can perform inspite of the functional limitations that have resulted from all of his/her impairments. It is important that the clinician's documentation of the RFC is detailed. SSA compares the RFC with the claimant's previous job requirements performed for the past 15 years. If the claimant has the ability to perform his/her past work, then the disability claim is denied.

The definition of RFC does not include what a claimant can do only occassionally. RFC is what a claimant can do "on a regular and continuing basis. . . . 8 hours a day, for 5 days a week, or an equivalent work schedule." (SSR 96-8p, 7/02/96[6]) For a more detailed explanation of RFC see APPENDIX B.

If the claimant possesses the functional capacity to perform past work, the claim is denied. Stop here. If the claimant does not possess the functional capacity to perform past work, proceed to Step five.

Step 5: Does the applicant have the residual functional capacity to perform any other work?

This final step in the evaluation process, involves the determination of whether or not the claimant can perform any other work. This step considers the age, education,

---

[6] http://www.socialsecurity.gov/OP_Home/rulings/di/01/SSR96-08-di-01.html.

literacy and work history of the claimant. Disability will be denied if other such jobs exist that the individual can perform.

"The term 'exertional' has the same meaning in the regulations as it has in the United States Department of Labor's publication, the Dictionary of Occupational Titles (DOT). In the DOT supplement, Selected Characteristics of Occupations Defined in the Dictionary of Occupational Titles (SCO), occupations are classified as sedentary, light, medium, heavy, and very heavy according to the degree of primary strength require-ments of the occupations. These consist of three work positions (standing, walking, and sitting) and four worker movements of objects (lifting, carrying, pushing, and pulling)."

Clinicians are encouraged to document functional limitations and activities the claimant can and cannot perform if the impairment does not meet the criteria used in the Social Security Administration's Listing of Impairments. This information is neces-sary for the SSA to make a determination of the claimant's residual functional capacity (RFC). RFC is maximum activity a claimant is able to perform despite the functional limitations resulting from the impairment. Once established, the RFC is compared to the work the claimant has performed for the past 15 years. If the claimant is capable of performing the work they have performed in the past 15 years, then the claim is denied.

SEE APPENDIX E

Using the Social Security Administration's Listing of Impairments

The listing of impairments found online.[7] It contains criteria that the Social Security Administration uses to evaluate and determine if a disability exists. This bluebook is intended predominately for health care professionals.

The listing of impairments describes impairments that are considered severe enough to prevent someone from engaging in gainful employment. The listing of impairments referred to here applies to adults eighteen years of age and over. This listing is broken down into fourteen major body systems and are as follows:

1.00 Musculoskeletal System

2.00 Special Senses and Speech

3.00 Respiratory System

4.00 Cardiovascular System

5.00 Digestive System

6.00 Genitourinary Disorders

7.00 Hematological Disorders

8.00 Skin Disorders

9.00 Endocrine System

10.00 Impairments that Affect Multiple Body Systems

11.00 Neurological

12.00 Mental Disorders

13.00 Malignant Neoplastic Diseases

14.00 Immune System

A favorable decision would require the claimant's medical condition meet one or more of these disabling conditions. This medical condition should be documented in the medical records with the diagnostic tests to prove this condition exists.

---

[7] http://www.socialsecurity.gov/disability/professionals/bluebook.

SSA's Description of The Listing Of Impairments

Medical Considerations

20 C.F.R. § 416.925 Listing of Impairments in Appendix 1 of Subpart P of Part 404

„What is the purpose of the Listing of Impairments? The Listing of Impairments (the listings) is in appendix 1 of subpart P of part 404 of this chapter. For adults, it describes for each of the major body systems impairments that we consider to be severe enough to prevent an individual from doing any gainful activity, regardless of his or her age, education, or work experience. For children, it describes impairments that cause marked and severe functional limitations.

(b) How is appendix 1 organized? There are two parts in appendix 1:

(1) Part A contains criteria that apply to individuals age 18 and over. We may also use part A for individuals who are under age 18 if the disease processes have a similar effect on adults and children.

(2)(i) Part B contains criteria that apply only to individuals who are under age 18; we never use the listings in part B to evaluate individuals who are age 18 or older. In evaluating disability for a person under age 18, we use part B first. If the criteria in part B do not apply, we may use the criteria in part A when those criteria give appropriate consideration to the effects of the impairment(s) in children. To the extent possible, we number the provisions in part B to maintain a relationship with their counterparts in part A.

(ii) Although the severity criteria in part B of the listings are expressed in different ways for different impairments, "listing-level severity" generally means the level of severity described in § 416.926a(a); that is, "marked" limitations in two domains of functioning or an "extreme" limitation in one domain. (See § 416.926a(e) for the definitions of the terms marked and extreme as they apply to children.) Therefore, in general, a child's impairment(s) is of "listing-level severity" if it causes marked limitations in two domains of functioning or an extreme limitation in one. However, when we decide whether your impairment(s) meets the requirements of a listing, we will decide that your impairment is of "listing-level severity" even if it does not result in marked limitations in two domains of functioning, or an extreme limitation in one, if the listing that we apply does not require such limitations to establish that an impairment(s) is disabling.

(c) How do we use the listings?

(1) Each body system section in parts A and B of appendix 1 of subpart P of part 404 of this chapter is in two parts: an introduction, followed by the specific listings.

(2) The introduction to each body system contains information relevant to the use of the listings in that body system; for example, examples of common impairments in the body system and definitions used in the listings for that body system. We may also include specific criteria for establishing a diagnosis, confirming the existence of an impairment, or establishing that your impairment(s) satisfies the criteria of a particular listing in the body system. Even if we do not include specific criteria for establishing a diagnosis or confirming the existence of your impairment, you must still show that you have a severe medically determinable impairment(s), as defined in §§ 416.908, 416.-920(c), and 416.924(c).

(3) The specific listings follow the introduction in each body system, after the heading, Category of Impairments. Within each listing, we specify the objective medical and other findings needed to satisfy the criteria of that listing. We will find that your impairment(s) meets the requirements of a listing when it satisfies all of the criteria of that listing, including any relevant criteria in the introduction, and meets the duration requirement (see § 416.909).

(4) Most of the listed impairments are permanent or expected to result in death. For some listings, we state a specific period of time for which your impairment(s) will meet the listing. For all others, the evidence must show that your impairment(s) has lasted or can be expected to last for a continuous period of at least 12 months.

(5) If your impairment(s) does not meet the criteria of a listing, it can medically equal the criteria of a listing. We explain our rules for medical equivalence in § 416.926. We use the listings only to find that you are disabled or still disabled. If your impairment(s) does not meet or medically equal the criteria of a listing, we may find that you are disabled or still disabled at a later step in the sequential evaluation process.

(d) Can your impairment(s) meet a listing based only on a diagnosis? No. Your impairment(s) cannot meet the criteria of a listing based only on a diagnosis. To meet the requirements of a listing, you must have a medically determinable impairment(s) that satisfies all of the criteria of the listing.

(e) How do we consider your symptoms when we determine whether your impairment(s) meets a listing? Some listed impairments include symptoms, such as pain, as criteria. Section 416.929(d)(2) explains how we consider your symptoms when your symptoms are included as criteria in a listing." [71 FR 10430, Mar. 1, 2006]

http://www.socialsecurity.gov/OP_Home/C.F.R.20/416/416-0925.htm

Who Can Document a Medical Impairment?

First, it is important to understand what the Social Security Administration considers to be a medical impairment. Second it is important to understand who the Social Security Administration considers qualified for the purposes of documenting an impairment for the purposes of supporting a disability claim. Third, it is important to understand the types of medical evidence that is required by the SSA in order to establish that an impairment exists.

The Social Security Administration defines a medically determinable impairment as "an impairment that results from anatomical, physiological, or psychological abnormalties which can be shown by medically acceptable clinical and laboratory diagnostic techniques." An impairment shall be confirmed by "medical evidence consisting of signs, symptoms, and laboratory findings - not only by the individuals statement of symptoms." (SSA Blue Book)

Documentation of the medical impairment must come from an acceptable medical source, as defined by the Social Security Administration. According to the Social Security Administration, an acceptable medical source means medical professionals, such as licensed physicians, licensed or certified psychologists, licensed optometrists, licensed podiatrists or qualified speech and language pathologists. (20 C.F.R. §§ 404.-1513 and 416.913 –see Appendixes C&D)

According to the Social Security Administration, the best medical evidence is obtained from the "treating source." A Treating source is a physician, or other acceptable medical source that has been providing treatment over an extended period of time. In other words there is an ongoing treatment relationship. One caveat though, the documented impairment that is addressed must be within the scope of his/her license or practice.

If the evidence provided by the claimant's medical care providers is insufficient to determine disability, then additional information may be requested from the treating clinician or a consultative examination from a different qualified medical source, may be required by the SSA.[8]

---

[8] http://www.ssa.gov/disability/professionals/greenbook/ce-guidelines. htm.

APPENDIX A

20 C.F.R. § 404.1526   Medical Equivalence

(a)   What is medical equivalence? Your impairment(s) is medically equivalent to a listed impairment in appendix 1 if it is at least equal in severity and duration to the criteria of any listed impairment.

(b)   How do we determine medical equivalence? We can find medical equivalence in three ways.

(1)   (i)   If you have an impairment that is described in appendix 1, but —
(A) You do not exhibit one or more of the findings specified in the particular listing, or
(B) You exhibit all of the findings, but one or more of the findings is not as severe as specified in the particular listing,
(ii) We will find that your impairment is medically equivalent to that listing if you have other findings related to your impairment that are at least of equal medical significance to the required criteria.

(2)   If you have an impairment(s) that is not described in appendix 1, we will compare your findings with those for closely analogous listed impairments. If the findings related to your impairment(s) are at least of equal medical significance to those of a listed impairment, we will find that your impairment(s) is medically equivalent to the analogous listing.

(3) If you have a combination of impairments, no one of which meets a listing (see § 404.1525(c)(3)), we will compare your findings with those for closely analogous listed impairments. If the findings related to your impairments are at least of equal medical significance to those of a listed impairment, we will find that your combination of impairments is medically equivalent to that listing.

(4)   Section 404.1529(d)(3) explains how we consider your symptoms, such as pain, when we make findings about medical equivalence.

(c)   What evidence do we consider when we determine if your impairment(s) medically equals a listing? When we determine if your impairment medically equals a listing, we consider all evidence in your case record about your impairment(s) and its effects on you that is relevant to this finding. We do not consider your vocational factors of age, education, and work experience (see, for example, § 404.1560 (c)(1)). We also consider the opinion given by one or more medical or psychological consultants designated by the Commissioner. (See § 404.1616.)

(d)   Who is a designated medical or psychological consultant? A medical or psychological consultant designated by the Commissioner includes any medical or psychological consultant employed or engaged to make medical judgments by the Social Security Administration, the Railroad Retirement Board, or a State agency authorized to make disability determinations, and includes a medical or psychological expert (as defined in § 405.5 of this chapter) in claims adjudicated under the procedures in part 405 of this chapter. A medical consultant must be an acceptable medical source identified in § 404.-1513(a)(1) or (a)(3) through (a)(5). A psychological consultant used in cases where there is evidence of a mental impairment must be a qualified psychologist. (See § 404.1616 for limitations on what medical consultants who are not physicians can evaluate and the qualifications we consider necessary for a psychologist to be a consultant.)

(e)   Who is responsible for determining medical equivalence? In cases where the State agency or other designee of the Commissioner makes the initial or reconsideration disability determination, a State agency medical or psychological consultant or other designee of the Commissioner (see § 404.1616) has the overall responsibility for determining medical equivalence. For cases in the disability hearing process or otherwise decided by a disability hearing officer, the responsibility for determining medical equivalence rests with either the disability hearing officer or, if the disability hearing officer's reconsideration determination is changed under § 404.918, with the Associate Commissioner for Disability Determinations or his or her delegate. For cases at the Administrative Law Judge or Appeals Council level, the responsibility for deciding medical equivalence rests with the Administrative Law Judge or Appeals Council.

[45 FR 55584, Aug. 20, 1980, as amended at 52 FR 33926, Sept. 9, 1987; 62 FR 38451, July 18, 1997; 65 FR 34957, June 1, 2000; 71 FR 10429, Mar. 1, 2006; 71 FR 16445, Mar. 31, 2006; 71 FR 57415, Sept. 29, 2006]

APPENDIX B

SSR 96-8p: Policy Interpretation Ruling Titles Ii and Xvi: Assessing Residual Functional Capacity in Initial Claims

PURPOSE: To state the Social Security Administration's policies and policy interpretations regarding the assessment of residual functional capacity (RFC) in initial claims for disability benefits under titles II and XVI of the Social Security Act (the Act). In particular, to emphasize that:

Ordinarily, RFC is an assessment of an individual's ability to do sustained work-related physical and mental activities in a work setting on a regular and continuing basis. A "regular and continuing basis" means 8 hours a day, for 5 days a week, or an equivalent work schedule.

The RFC assessment considers only functional limitations and restrictions that result from an individual's medically determinable impairment or combination of impairments, including the impact of any related symptoms. Age and body habitus are not factors in assessing RFC. It is incorrect to find that an individual has limitations beyond those caused by his or her medically determinable impairment(s) and any related symptoms, due to such factors as age and natural body build, and the activities the individual was accustomed to doing in his or her previous work.

When there is no allegation of a physical or mental limitation or restriction of a specific functional capacity, and no information in the case record that there is such a limitation or restriction, the adjudicator must consider the individual to have no limitation or restriction with respect to that functional capacity.

The RFC assessment must first identify the individual's functional limitations or restrictions and assess his or her work-related abilities on a function-by-function basis, including the functions in paragraphs (b), (c), and (d) of 20 C.F.R. §§ 404.1545 and 416.-945. Only after that may RFC be expressed in terms of the exertional levels of work, sedentary, light, medium, heavy, and very heavy.

RFC is not the least an individual can do despite his or her limitations or restrictions, but the most.

Medical impairments and symptoms, including pain, are not intrinsically exertional or nonexertional. It is the functional limitations or restrictions caused by medical impairments and their related symptoms that are categorized as exertional or nonexer-

18

tional.

AUTHORITY: Sections 223(d) and 1614(a) of the Social Security Act, as amended; Regulations No. 4, subpart P, sections 404.1513, 404.1520, 404.1520a, 404.1545, 404.1546, 404.1560, 404.1561, 404.1569a, and appendix 2; and Regulations No. 16, subpart I, sections 416.913, 416.920, 416.920a, 416.945, 416.946, 416.960, 416.961, and 416.969a.

INTRODUCTION: In disability determinations and decisions made at steps 4 and 5 of the sequential evaluation process in 20 C.F.R. 404.1520 and 416.920, in which the individual's ability to do past relevant work and other work must be considered, the adjudicator must assess RFC. This Ruling clarifies the term "RFC" and discusses the elements considered in the assessment. It describes concepts for both physical and mental RFC assessments.

This Ruling applies to the assessment of RFC in claims for initial entitlement to disability benefits under titles II and XVI. Although most rules and procedures regarding RFC assessment in deciding whether an individual's disability continues are the same, there are some differences.

POLICY INTERPRETATION:

GENERAL

When an individual is not engaging in substantial gainful activity and a determination or decision cannot be made on the basis of medical factors alone (i.e., when the impairment is severe because it has more than a minimal effect on the ability to do basic work activities yet does not meet or equal in severity the requirements of any impairment in the Listing of Impairments), the sequential evaluation process generally must continue with an identification of the individual's functional limitations and restrictions and an assessment of his or her remaining capacities for work-related activities.[9] This assessment of RFC is used at step 4 of the sequential evaluation process

---

[9] However, a finding of "disabled" will be made for an individual who: a) has a severe impairment(s), b) has no past relevant work, c) is age 55 or older, and d) has no more than a limited education. (See SSR 82-63 "Titles II and XVI: Medical- Vocational Profiles Showing an Inability to Make an Adjustment to Other Work" (C.E. 1981-1985, p. 447.) In such a case, it is not necessary to assess the individual's RFC to determine if he or

to determine whether an individual is able to do past relevant work, and at step 5 to determine whether an individual is able to do other work, considering his or her age, education, and work experience.

Definition of RFC. RFC is what an individual can still do despite his or her limitations. RFC is an administrative assessment of the extent to which an individual's medically determinable impairment(s), including any related symptoms, such as pain, may cause physical or mental limitations or restrictions that may affect his or her capacity to do work-related physical and mental activities. (See SSR 96-4p, "Titles II and XVI: Symptoms, Medically Determinable Physical and Mental Impairments, and Exertional and Nonexertional Limitations.") Ordinarily, RFC is the individual's maximum remaining ability to do sustained work activities in an ordinary work setting on a regular and continuing basis, and the RFC assessment must include a discussion of the individual's abilities on that basis. A "regular and continuing basis" means 8 hours a day, for 5 days a week, or an equivalent work schedule.[10] RFC does not represent the least an individual can do despite his or her limitations or restrictions, but the most.[11] RFC is assessed by adjudicators at each level of the administrative review process based on all of the relevant evidence in the case record, including information about the individual's symptoms and any "medical source statements" — i.e., opinions about what the individual can still do despite his or her impairment(s) — submitted by an individual's treating source or other acceptable medical sources.[12]

---

she meets this special profile and is, therefore, disabled.

[10] The ability to work 8 hours a day for 5 days a week is not always required when evaluating an individual's ability to do past relevant work at step 4 of the sequential evaluation process. Part-time work that was substantial gainful activity, performed within the past 15 years, and lasted long enough for the person to learn to do it constitutes past relevant work, and an individual who retains the RFC to perform such work must be found not disabled.

[11]See SSR 83-10, "Titles II and XVI: Determining Capability to Do Other Work-- The Medical Vocational Rules of Appendix 2" (C.E. 1981-1985, p. 516). SSR 83-10 states that "(T)he RFC determines a work capability that is exertionally sufficient to allow performance of at least substantially all of the activities of work at a particular level (e.g., sedentary, light, or medium), but is also insufficient to allow substantial performance of work at greater exertional levels."

[12]For a detailed discussion of the difference between the RFC assessment, which is an administrative finding of fact, and the opinion evidence called the "medical source

The RFC Assessment Must be Based Solely on the Individual's Impairment(s). The Act requires that an individual's inability to work must result from the individual's physical or mental impairment(s). Therefore, in assessing RFC, the adjudicator must consider only limitations and restrictions attributable to medically determinable impairments. It is incorrect to find that an individual has limitations or restrictions beyond those caused by his or her medical impairment(s) including any related symptoms, such as pain, due to factors such as age or height, or whether the individual had ever engaged in certain activities in his or her past relevant work (e.g., lifting heavy weights.) Age and body habitus (i.e., natural body build, physique, constitution, size, and weight, insofar as they are unrelated to the individual's medically determinable impairment(s) and related symptoms) are not factors in assessing RFC in initial claims.[13]

Likewise, when there is no allegation of a physical or mental limitation or restriction of a specific functional capacity, and no information in the case record that there is such a limitation or restriction, the adjudicator must consider the individual to have no limitation or restriction with respect to that functional capacity.

---

statement" or "MSS," see SSR 96-5p, "Titles II and XVI: Medical Source Opinions on Issues Reserved to the Commissioner."

[13]The definition of disability in the Act requires that an individual's inability to work must be due to a medically determinable physical or mental impairment(s). The assessment of RFC must therefore be concerned with the impact of a disease process or injury on the individual. In determining a person's maximum RFC for sustained activity, factors of age or body habitus must not be allowed to influence the assessment.

RFC AND SEQUENTIAL EVALUATION

RFC is an issue only at steps 4 and 5 of the sequential evaluation process. The following are issues regarding the RFC assessment and its use at each of these steps.

RFC and exertional levels of work. The RFC assessment is a function-by-function assessment based upon all of the relevant evidence of an individual's ability to do work-related activities. At step 4 of the sequential evaluation process, the RFC must not be expressed initially in terms of the exertional categories of "sedentary," "light," "medium," "heavy," and "very heavy" work because the first consideration at this step is whether the individual can do past relevant work as he or she actually performed it.

RFC may be expressed in terms of an exertional category, such as light, if it becomes necessary to assess whether an individual is able to do his or her past relevant work as it is generally performed in the national economy. However, without the initial function-by- function assessment of the individual's physical and mental capacities, it may not be possible to determine whether the individual is able to do past relevant work as it is generally performed in the national economy because particular occupations may not require all of the exertional and nonexertional demands necessary to do the full range of work at a given exertional level.

At step 5 of the sequential evaluation process, RFC must be expressed in terms of, or related to, the exertional categories when the adjudicator determines whether there is other work the individual can do. However, in order for an individual to do a full range of work at a given exertional level, such as sedentary, the individual must be able to perform substantially all of the exertional and nonexertional functions required in work at that level. Therefore, it is necessary to assess the individual s capacity to perform each of these functions in order to decide which exertional level is appropriate and whether the individual is capable of doing the full range of work contemplated by the exertional level.

Initial failure to consider an individual's ability to perform the specific work-related functions could be critical to the outcome of a case. For example:

At step 4 of the sequential evaluation process, it is especially important to determine whether an individual who is at least "closely approaching advanced age" is able to do past relevant work because failure to address this issue at step 4 can result in an erroneous finding that the individual is disabled at step 5. It is very important to consider first whether the individual can still do past relevant work as he or she actually performed it because individual jobs within an occupational category as performed for particular employers may not entail all of the requirements of the exertional level indicated for that category in the Dictionary of Occupational Titles and its related volumes.

The opposite result may also occur at step 4 of the sequential evaluation process. When it is found that an individual cannot do past relevant work as he or she actually performed it, the adjudicator must consider whether the individual can do the work as it is generally performed in the national economy. Again, however, a failure to first make a function-by-function assessment of the individual's limitations or restrictions could result in the adjudicator overlooking some of an individual's limitations or restrictions. This could lead to an incorrect use of an exertional category to find that the individual is able to do past relevant work as it is generally performed and an erroneous finding that the individual is not disabled.

At step 5 of the sequential evaluation process, the same failures could result in an improper application of the rules in appendix 2 to subpart P of the Regulations No. 4 (the "Medical-Vocational Guidelines) and could make the difference between a finding of "disabled" and "not disabled." Without a careful consideration of an individual's functional capacities to support an RFC assessment based on an exertional category, the adjudicator may either overlook limitations or restrictions that would narrow the ranges and types of work an individual may be able to do, or find that the individual has limitations or restrictions that he or she does not actually have.

RFC represents the most that an individual can do despite his or her limitations or restrictions. At step 5 of the sequential evaluation process, RFC must not be expressed in terms of the lowest exertional level (e.g., "sedentary" or "light" when the individual can perform "medium" work) at which the medical-vocational rules would still direct a finding of "not disabled." This would concede lesser functional abilities than the individual actually possesses and would not reflect the most he or she can do based on the evidence in the case record, as directed by the regulations.[14]

---

[14]In the Fourth Circuit, adjudicators are required to adopt a finding, absent new and material evidence, regarding the individual's RFC made in a final decision by an administrative law judge or the Appeals Council on a prior disability claim arising under the same title of the Act. In this jurisdiction, an unfavorable determination or decision using the lowest exertional level at which the rules would direct a finding of not disabled could result in an unwarranted favorable determination or decision on an individual's subsequent application; for example, if the individual's age changes to a higher age category following the final decision on the earlier application. See Acquiescence Ruling

The psychiatric review technique. The psychiatric review technique described in 20 C.F.R. 404.1520a and 416.920a and summarized on the Psychiatric Review Technique Form (PRTF) requires adjudicators to assess an individual's limitations and restrictions from a mental impairment(s) in categories identified in the "paragraph B" and "paragraph C" criteria of the adult mental disorders listings. The adjudicator must remember that the limitations identified in the "paragraph B" and "paragraph C" criteria are not an RFC assessment but are used to rate the severity of mental impairment(s) at steps 2 and 3 of the sequential evaluation process. The mental RFC assessment used at steps 4 and 5 of the sequential evaluation process requires a more detailed assessment by itemizing various functions contained in the broad categories found in paragraphs B and C of the adult mental disorders listings in 12.00 of the Listing of Impairments, and summarized on the PRTF.

(AR) 94-2(4), "Lively v. Secretary of Health and Human Services, 820 F.2d 1391 (4th Cir. 1987)--Effect of Prior Disability Findings on Adjudication of a Subsequent Disability Claim Arising Under the Same Title of the Social Security Act--Titles II and XVI of the Social Security Act." AR 94-2(4) applies to disability findings in cases involving claimants who reside in the Fourth Circuit at the time of the determination or decision on the subsequent claim.

EVIDENCE CONSIDERED

The RFC assessment must be based on all of the relevant evidence in the case record, such as:

Medical history;

Medical signs and laboratory findings;

The effects of treatment, including limitations or restrictions imposed by the mechanics of treatment (e.g., frequency of treatment, duration, disruption to routine, side effects of medication);

Reports of daily activities;

Lay evidence;

Recorded observations;

Medical source statements;

Effects of symptoms, including pain, that are reasonably attributed to a medically determinable impairment;

Evidence from attempts to work;

Need for a structured living environment; and,

Work evaluations, if available.

The adjudicator must consider all allegations of physical and mental limitations or restrictions and make every reasonable effort to ensure that the file contains sufficient evidence to assess RFC. Careful consideration must be given to any available information about symptoms because subjective descriptions may indicate more severe limitations or restrictions than can be shown by objective medical evidence alone.

In assessing RFC, the adjudicator must consider limitations and restrictions imposed by all of an individual's impairments, even those that are not "severe." While a "not severe" impairment(s) standing alone may not significantly limit an individual's ability to do basic work activities, it may–when considered with limitations or restrictions due to other impairments– be critical to the outcome of a claim. For example, in combination with limitations imposed by an individual's other impairments, the limitations due to such a "not severe" impairment may prevent an individual from performing past relevant work or may narrow the range of other work that the individual may still be able to do.

EXERTIONAL AND NONEXERTIONAL FUNCTIONS

The RFC assessment must address both the remaining exertional and nonexertional capacities of the individual.

Exertional capacity

Exertional capacity addresses an individual's limitations and restrictions of physical strength and defines the individual's remaining abilities to perform each of seven strength demands: Sitting, standing, walking, lifting, carrying, pushing, and pulling. Each function must be considered separately (e.g., "the individual can walk for 5 out of 8 hours and stand for 6 out of 8 hours"), even if the final RFC assessment will combine activities (e.g., "walk/stand, lift/ carry, push/ pull"). Although the regulations describing the exertional levels of work and the Dictionary of Occupational Titles and its related volumes pair some functions, it is not invariably the case that treating the activities together will result in the same decisional outcome as treating them separately.

It is especially important that adjudicators consider the capacities separately when deciding whether an individual can do past relevant work. However, separate consideration may also influence decisionmaking at step 5 of the sequential evaluation process, for reasons already given in the section on "RFC and Sequential Evaluation."

Nonexertional capacity

Nonexertional capacity considers all work-related limitations and restrictions that do not depend on an individual's physical strength; i.e., all physical limitations and restrictions that are not reflected in the seven strength demands, and mental limitations and restrictions. It assesses an individual's abilities to perform physical activities such as postural (e.g., stooping, climbing), manipulative (e.g., reaching, handling), visual (seeing), communicative (hearing, speaking), and mental (e.g., understanding and remembering instructions and responding appropriately to supervision). In addition to these activities, it also considers the ability to tolerate various environmental factors (e.g., tolerance of temperature extremes).

As with exertional capacity, nonexertional capacity must be expressed in terms of work- related functions. For example, in assessing RFC for an individual with a visual impairment, the adjudicator must consider the individual's residual capacity to perform such work-related functions as working with large or small objects, following instructions, or avoiding ordinary hazards in the workplace. In assessing RFC with impairments affecting hearing or speech, the adjudicator must explain how the individual's limitations would affect his or her ability to communicate in the workplace. Work-related mental activities generally required by competitive, remunerative work include the abilities to: understand, carry out, and remember instructions; use judgment in making work-related decisions; respond appropriately to supervision, co-workers and work situations; and deal with changes in a routine work setting.

Consider the nature of the activity affected

It is the nature of an individual's limitations or restrictions that determines whether the individual will have only exertional limitations or restrictions, only nonexertional limitations or restrictions, or a combination of exertional and nonexertional limitations or restrictions. For example, symptoms, including pain, are not intrinsically exertional or nonexertional. Symptoms often affect the capacity to perform one of the seven strength demands and may or may not have effects on the demands of occupations other than the strength demands.

If the only limitations or restrictions caused by symptoms, such as pain, are in one or more of the seven strength demands (e.g., lifting) the limitations or restrictions will be exertional. On the other hand, if an individual's symptoms cause a limitation or restriction that affects the individual's ability to meet the demands of occupations other than their strength demands (e.g., manipulation or concentration), the limitation or restriction will be classified as nonexertional. Symptoms may also cause both exertional and nonexertional limitations.

Likewise, even though mental impairments usually affect nonexertional functions, they may also limit exertional capacity by affecting one or more of the seven strength demands. For example, a mental impairment may cause fatigue or hysterical paralysis.

NARRATIVE DISCUSSION REQUIREMENTS

The RFC assessment must include a narrative discussion describing how the evidence supports each conclusion, citing specific medical facts (e.g., laboratory findings) and nonmedical evidence (e.g., daily activities, observations). In assessing RFC, the adjudicator must discuss the individual's ability to perform sustained work activities in an ordinary work setting on a regular and continuing basis (i.e., 8 hours a day, for 5 days a week, or an equivalent work schedule)[15], and describe the maximum amount of each work-related activity the individual can perform based on the evidence available in the case record. The adjudicator must also explain how any material inconsistencies or ambiguities in the evidence in the case record were considered and resolved.

Symptoms. In all cases in which symptoms, such as pain, are alleged, the RFC assessment must:

> Contain a thorough discussion and analysis of the objective medical and other evidence, including the individual's complaints of pain and other symptoms and the adjudicator's personal observations, if appropriate;

> Include a resolution of any inconsistencies in the evidence as a whole; and

> Set forth a logical explanation of the effects of the symptoms,

---

[15] See Footnote 2.

including pain, on the individual's ability to work.

The RFC assessment must include a discussion of why reported symptom-related functional limitations and restrictions can or cannot reasonably be accepted as consistent with the medical and other evidence. In instances in which the adjudicator has observed the individual, he or she is not free to accept or reject that individual's complaints solely on the basis of such personal observations. (For further information about RFC assessment and the evaluation of symptoms, see SSR 96-7p, "Titles II and XVI: Evaluation of Symptoms in Disability Claims: Assessing the Credibility of an Individual's Statements.")

Medical opinions. The RFC assessment must always consider and address medical source opinions. If the RFC assessment conflicts with an opinion from a medical source, the adjudicator must explain why the opinion was not adopted.

Medical opinions from treating sources about the nature and severity of an individual's impairment(s) are entitled to special significance and may be entitled to controlling weight. If a treating source's medical opinion on an issue of the nature and severity of an individual's impairment(s) is well-supported by medically acceptable clinical and laboratory diagnostic techniques and is not inconsistent with the other substantial evidence in the case record, the adjudicator must give it controlling weight. (See SSR 96-2p, "Titles II and XVI: Giving Controlling Weight to Treating Source Medical Opinions," and SSR 96-5p, "Titles II and XVI: Medical Source Opinions on Issues Reserved to the Commissioner.")[16]

CROSS-REFERENCES: SSR 82-52, "Titles II and XVI: Duration of the Impairment"

---

[16] A medical source opinion that an individual is "disabled" or "unable to work," has an impairment(s) that meets or is equivalent in severity to the requirements of a listing, has a particular RFC, or that concerns the application of vocational factors, is an opinion on an issue reserved to the Commissioner. Every such opinion must still be considered in adjudicating a disability claim; however, the adjudicator will not give any special significance to the opinion because of its source. See SSR 96-5p, "Titles II and XVI: Medical Source Opinions on Issues Reserved to the Commissioner." For further information about the evaluation of medical source opinions, SSR 96-6p, "Titles II and XVI: Consideration of Administrative Findings of Fact by State Agency Medical and Psychological Consultants and Other Program Physicians and Psychologists at the Administrative Law Judge and Appeals Council Levels of Administrative Review; Medical Equivalence."

(C.E. 1981-1985, p. 328), SSR 82-61, "Titles II and XVI: Past Relevant Work—The Particular Job Or the Occupation As Generally Performed" (C.E. 1981-1985, p. 427), SSR 82-62, "Titles II and XVI: A Disability Claimant's Capacity To Do Past Relevant Work, In General" (C.E. 1981-1985, p. 400), SSR 83-20, "Titles II and XVI: Onset of Disability" (C.E. 1981-1985, p. 375), SSR 85-16, "Titles II and XVI: Residual Functional Capacity for Mental Impairments" (C.E. 1981- 1985, p. 390), SSR 86-8, "Titles II and XVI: The Sequential Evaluation Process" (C.E. 1986, p. 78), SSR 96-6p, "Titles II and XVI: Consideration of Administrative Findings of Fact by State Agency Medical and Psychological Consultants and Other Program Physicians and Psychologists at the Administrative Law Judge and Appeals Council Levels of Administrative Review; Medical Equivalence," SSR 96-2p, "Titles II and XVI: Giving Controlling Weight to Treating Source Medical Opinions," SSR 96-4p, "Titles II and XVI: Symptoms, Medically Determinable Physical and Mental Impairments, and Exertional and Nonexertional Limitations," SSR 96-5p "Titles II and XVI: Medical Source Opinions on Issues Reserved to the Commissioner," SSR 96-9p "Titles II and XVI: Determining Capability to Do Other Work--Implications of a Residual Functional Capacity for Less Than a Full Range of Sedentary Work," SSR 96-7p, "Titles II and XVI: Evaluation of Symptoms in Disability Claims: Assessing the Credibility of an Individual's Statements;" and Program Operations Manual System, sections DI 22515.010, DI 24510.000 ff., DI 24515.002, DI 24515. 007, DI 24515.061, DI 24515.062, DI 24515.064, DI 25501.000 ff., DI 25505.000 ff., and DI 28015.000 ff.

APPENDIX C

20 C.F.R. §404.1513 Medical and Other Evidence of Your Impairment(s)

(a)	Sources who can provide evidence to establish an impairment. We need evidence from acceptable medical sources to establish whether you have a medically determinable impairment(s). See § 404.1508. Acceptable medical sources are —

(1)	Licensed physicians (medical or osteopathic doctors);

(2)	Licensed or certified psychologists. Included are school psychologists, or other licensed or certified individuals with other titles who perform the same function as a school psychologist in a school setting, for purposes of establishing mental retardation, learning disabilities, and borderline intellectual functioning only;

(3)	Licensed optometrists, for purposes of establishing visual disorders only (except, in the U.S. Virgin Islands, licensed optometrists, for the measurement of visual acuity and visual fields only);

(4)	Licensed podiatrists, for purposes of establishing impairments of the foot, or foot and ankle only, depending on whether the State in which the podiatrist practices permits the practice of podiatry on the foot only, or the foot and ankle; and

(5)	Qualified speech-language pathologists, for purposes of establishing speech or language impairments only. For this source, "qualified" means that the speech-language pathologist must be licensed by the State professional licensing agency, or be fully certified by the State education agency in the State in which he or she practices, or hold a Certificate of Clinical Competence from the American Speech-Language- Hearing Association.

(b)	Medical reports. Medical reports should include —

(1)	Medical history;

(2)	Clinical findings (such as the results of physical or mental status examinations);

(3)	Laboratory findings (such as blood pressure, x-rays);

(4)	Diagnosis (statement of disease or injury based on its signs and symptoms);

(5)	Treatment prescribed with response, and prognosis; and

(6)	A statement about what you can still do despite your impairment(s) based on the acceptable medical source's findings on the factors under paragraphs (b)(1) through (b)(5) of this section (except in statutory blindness claims). Although we will request a medical source statement about what you can still do despite your impairment(s), the lack of the medical source statement will not make the report incomplete. See § 404.1527.

(c)   Statements about what you can still do. At the administrative law judge and Appeals Council levels, and at the reviewing official, administrative law judge, and Decision Review Board levels in claims adjudicated under the procedures in part 405 of this chapter, we will consider residual functional capacity assessments made by State agency medical and psychological consultants, medical and psychological experts (as defined in § 405.5 of this chapter), and other program physicians and psychologists to be "statements about what you can still do" made by nonexamining physicians and psychologists based on their review of the evidence in the case record. Statements about what you can still do (based on the acceptable medical source's findings on the factors under paragraphs (b)(1) through (b)(5) of this section) should describe, but are not limited to, the kinds of physical and mental capabilities listed as follows (See §§ 404.1527 and 404.1545(c)):

(1)   The acceptable medical source's opinion about your ability, despite your impairment(s), to do work-related activities such as sitting, standing, walking, lifting, carrying, handling objects, hearing, speaking, and traveling; and

(2)   In cases of mental impairment(s), the acceptable medical source's opinion about your ability to understand, to carry out and remember instructions, and to respond appropriately to supervision, coworkers, and work pressures in a work setting.

(d)   Other sources. In addition to evidence from the acceptable medical sources listed in paragraph (a) of this section, we may also use evidence from other sources to show the severity of your impairment(s) and how it affects your ability to work. Other sources include, but are not limited to—

(1)   Medical sources not listed in paragraph (a) of this section (for example, nurse-practitioners, physicians' assistants, naturopaths, chiropractors, audiologists, and therapists);

(2)   Educational personnel (for example, school teachers, counselors, early intervention team members, developmental center workers, and daycare center workers);

(3)   Public and private social welfare agency personnel; and

(4)   Other non-medical sources (for example, spouses, parents and other caregivers, siblings, other relatives, friends, neighbors, and clergy).

(e)   Completeness. The evidence in your case record, including the medical evidence from acceptable medical sources (containing the clinical and laboratory findings) and other medical sources not listed in paragraph (a) of this section, information you give us about your medical condition(s) and how it affects you, and other evidence from other sources, must be complete and detailed enough to allow us to make a determination or decision about whether you are disabled or blind. It must allow us to determine—

 (1) The nature and severity of your impairment(s) for any period in question;

 (2) Whether the duration requirement described in § 404.1509 is met; and

 (3) Your residual functional capacity to do work-related physical and mental activities, when the evaluation steps described in § 404.1520 (e) or (f)(1) apply.

[45 FR 55584, Aug. 20, 1980, as amended at 56 FR 36955, Aug. 1, 1991; 65 FR 11875, Mar. 7, 2000; 65 FR 34957, June 1, 2000; 71 FR 16444, Mar. 31, 2006; 72 FR 9242, Mar. 1, 2007]

APPENDIX D

20 C.F.R. § 416.913 Medical and Other Evidence of Your Impairments

(a)　　Sources who can provide evidence to establish an impairment. We need evidence from acceptable medical sources to establish whether you have a medically determinable impairment(s). See § 416.908. Acceptable medical sources are—

(1)　　Licensed physicians (medical or osteopathic doctors);

(2)　　Licensed or certified psychologists. Included are school psychologists, or other licensed or certified individuals with other titles who perform the same function as a school psychologist in a school setting, for purposes of establishing mental retardation, learning disabilities, and borderline intellectual functioning only;

(3)　　Licensed optometrists, for purposes of establishing visual disorders only (except, in the U.S. Virgin Islands, licensed optometrists, for the measurement of visual acuity and visual fields only). (See paragraph (f) of this section for the evidence needed for statutory blindness);

(4)　　Licensed podiatrists, for purposes of establishing impairments of the foot, or foot and ankle only, depending on whether the State in which the podiatrist practices permits the practice of podiatry on the foot only, or the foot and ankle; and

(5)　　Qualified speech-language pathologists, for purposes of establishing speech or language impairments only. For this source, "qualified" means that the speech-language pathologist must be licensed by the State professional licensing agency, or be fully certified by the State education agency in the State in which he or she practices, or hold a Certificate of Clinical Competence from the American-Speech-Language-Hearing Association.

(b)　　Medical reports. Medical reports should include—

(1)　　Medical history;

(2)　　Clinical findings (such as the results of physical or mental status examinations);

(3)　　Laboratory findings (such as blood pressure, X-rays);

(4)　　Diagnosis (statement of disease or injury based on its signs and symptoms);

(5)　　Treatment prescribed with response, and prognosis; and

(6)　　A statement about what you can still do despite your impairment(s) based on the acceptable medical source's findings on the factors under paragraphs (b)(1) through (b)(5) of this section (except in statutory blindness claims). Although we will request a medical source statement about what you can still do despite your impairment(s), the lack of the medical source statement will not make the report incomplete. See § 416.927.

(c)   Statements about what you can still do. At the administrative law judge and Appeals Council levels, and at the reviewing official, administrative law judge, and Decision Review Board levels in claims adjudicated under the procedures in part 405 of this chapter, we will consider residual functional capacity assessments made by State agency medical and psychological consultants, medical and psychological experts (as defined in § 405.5 of this chapter), and other program physicians and psychologists to be "statements about what you can still do" made by nonexamining physicians and psychologists based on their review of the evidence in the case record. Statements about what you can still do (based on the acceptable medical source's findings on the factors under paragraphs (b)(1) through (b)(5) of this section) should describe, but are not limited to, the kinds of physical and mental capabilities listed as follows (See §§ 416.927 and 416.945(c)):

(1)   If you are an adult, the acceptable medical source's opinion about your ability, despite your impairment(s), to do work-related activities such as sitting, standing, walking, lifting, carrying, handling objects, hearing, speaking, and traveling;

(2)   If you are an adult, in cases of mental impairment(s), the acceptable medical source's opinion about your ability to understand, to carry out and remember instructions, and to respond appropriately to supervision, coworkers, and work pressures in a work setting; and

(3)   If you are a child, the medical source's opinion about your functional limitations compared to children your age who do not have impairments in acquiring and using information, attending and completing tasks, interacting and relating with others, moving about and manipulating objects, caring for yourself, and health and physical well-being.

(d)   Other sources. In addition to evidence from the acceptable medical sources listed in paragraph (a) of this section, we may also use evidence from other sources to show the severity of your impairment(s) and how it affects your ability to work or, if you are a child, how you typically function compared to children your age who do not have impairments. Other sources include, but are not limited to—

(1)   Medical sources not listed in paragraph (a) of this section (for example, nurse-practitioners, physicians' assistants, naturopaths, chiropractors, audiologists, and therapists);

(2)   Educational personnel (for example, school teachers, counselors, early intervention team members, developmental center workers, and daycare center workers);

(3)   Public and private social welfare agency personnel; and

(4)   Other non-medical sources (for example, spouses, parents and other caregivers, siblings, other relatives, friends, neighbors, and clergy).

(e)   Completeness. The evidence in your case record, including the medical evidence from acceptable medical sources (containing the clinical and laboratory findings) and other medical sources not listed in paragraph (a) of this section, information you give us about your medical condition(s) and how it affects you, and other evidence from other sources, must be complete and detailed enough to allow us to make a determination or decision about whether you are disabled or blind. It must allow us to determine—

(1)   The nature and severity of your impairment(s) for any period in question;

(2)   Whether the duration requirement described in § 416.909 is met; and

(3)   Your residual functional capacity to do work-related physical and mental activities, when the evaluation steps described in § 416.920 (e) or (f)(1) apply, or, if you are a child, how you typically function compared to children your age who do not have impairments.

(f)   Evidence we need to establish statutory blind ness. If you are applying for benefits on the basis of statutory blindness, we will require an examination by a physician skilled in diseases of the eye or by an optometrist, whichever you may select.

[45 FR 55621, Aug. 20, 1980, as amended at 56 FR 5553, Feb. 11, 1991; 56 FR 36964, Aug. 1, 1991; 58 FR 47577, Sept. 9, 1993; 62 FR 6421, Feb. 11, 1997; 65 FR 11878, Mar. 7, 2000; 65 FR 34958, June 1, 2000; 65 FR 54777, Sept. 11, 2000; 71 FR 16459, Mar. 31, 2006; 72 FR 9242, Mar. 1, 2007]

APPENDIX E

Code of Federal Regulations 20 Appendix 2 to Subpart P of Part 404 — Medical Vocational Guidelines

200.00 Introduction.

201.00 Maximum sustained work capability limited to sedentary work as a result of severe medically determinable impairment(s).

202.00 Maximum sustained work capability limited to light work as a result of severe medically determinable impairment(s).

203.00 Maximum sustained work capability limited to medium work as a result of severe medically determinable impairment(s).

204.00 Maximum sustained work capability limited to heavy work (or very heavy work) as a result of severe medically determinable impairment(s).

200.00 Introduction

(a) The following rules reflect the major functional and vocational patterns which are encountered in cases which cannot be evaluated on medical considerations alone, where an individual with a severe medically determinable physical or mental impairment(s) is not engaging in substantial gainful activity and the individual's impairment(s) prevents the performance of his or her vocationally relevant past work. They also reflect the analysis of the various vocational factors (i.e., age, education, and work experience) in combination with the individual's residual functional capacity (used to determine his or her maximum sustained work capability for sedentary, light, medium, heavy, or very heavy work) in evaluating the individual's ability to engage in substantial gainful activity in other than his or her vocationally relevant past work. Where the findings of fact made with respect to a particular individual's vocational factors and residual functional capacity coincide with all of the criteria of a particular rule, the rule directs a conclusion as to whether the individual is or is not disabled. However, each of these findings of fact is subject to rebuttal and the individual may present evidence to refute such findings. Where any one of the findings of fact does not coincide with the corresponding criterion of a rule, the rule does not apply in that particular case and, accordingly, does not direct a conclusion of disabled or not disabled.

In any instance where a rule does not apply, full consideration must be given to all of the relevant facts of the case in accordance with the definitions and discussions of each factor in the appropriate sections of the regulations.

(b) The existence of jobs in the national economy is reflected in the "Decisions" shown in the rules; i.e., in promulgating the rules, administrative notice has been taken of the numbers of unskilled jobs that exist throughout the national economy at the various functional levels (sedentary, light, medium, heavy, and very heavy) as supported by the "Dictionary of Occupational Titles" and the "Occupational Outlook Handbook," published by the Department of Labor; the "County Business Patterns" and "Census Surveys" published by the Bureau of the Census; and occupational surveys of light and sedentary jobs prepared for the Social Security Administration by various State employment agencies. Thus, when all factors coincide with the criteria of a rule, the existence of such jobs is established. However, the existence of such jobs for individuals whose remaining functional capacity or other factors do not coincide with the criteria of a rule must be further considered in terms of what kinds of jobs or types of work may be either additionally indicated or precluded.

(c) In the application of the rules, the individual's residual functional capacity (i.e., the maximum degree to which the individual retains the capacity for sustained performance of the physical-mental requirements of jobs), age, education, and work experience must first be determined. When assessing the person's residual functional capacity, we consider his or her symptoms (such as pain), signs, and laboratory findings together with other evidence we obtain.

(d) The correct disability decision (i.e., on the issue of ability to engage in substantial gainful activity) is found by then locating the individual's specific vocational profile. If an individual's specific profile is not listed within this appendix 2, a conclusion of disabled or not disabled is not directed. Thus, for example, an individual's ability to engage in substantial gainful work where his or her residual functional capacity falls between the ranges of work indicated in the rules (e.g., the individual who can perform more than light but less than medium work), is decided on the basis of the principles and definitions in the regulations, giving consideration to the rules for specific case situations in this appendix 2. These rules represent various combinations of exertional capabilities, age, education and work experience and also provide an overall structure for evaluation of those cases in which the judgments as to each factor do not coincide with those of any specific rule. Thus, when the necessary judgments have been made as to each factor and it is found that no specific rule applies, the rules still provide guidance for decision making, such as in cases involving combinations of impairments. For example, if strength limitations resulting from an individual's impairment(s) considered with the judgments made as to the individual's age, education and work experience correspond to (or closely approximate) the factors of a particular rule, the adjudicator then has a frame of reference for considering the jobs or types of work precluded by other, nonexertional impairments in terms of numbers of jobs remaining for a particular individual.

(e)   Since the rules are predicated on an individual's having an impairment which manifests itself by limitations in meeting the strength requirements of jobs, they may not be fully applicable where the nature of an individual's impairment does not result in such limitations, e.g., certain mental, sensory, or skin impairments. In addition, some impairments may result solely in postural and manipulative limitations or environmental restrictions. Environmental restrictions are those restrictions which result in inability to tolerate some physical feature(s) of work settings that occur in certain industries or types of work, e.g., an inability to tolerate dust or fumes.

(1)   In the evaluation of disability where the individual has solely a nonexertional type of impairment, determination as to whether disability exists shall be based on the principles in the appropriate sections of the regulations, giving consideration to the rules for specific case situations in this appendix 2. The rules do not direct factual conclusions of disabled or not disabled for individuals with solely nonexertional types of impairments.

(2)   However, where an individual has an impairment or combination of impairments resulting in both strength limitations and nonexertional limitations, the rules in this subpart are considered in determining first whether a finding of disabled may be possible based on the strength limitations alone and, if not, the rule(s) reflecting the individual's maximum residual strength capabilities, age, education, and work experience provide a framework for consideration of how much the individual's work capability is further diminished in terms of any types of jobs that would be contraindicated by the nonexertional limitations. Also, in these combinations of nonexertional and exertional limitations which cannot be wholly determined under the rules in this appendix 2, full consideration must be given to all of the relevant facts in the case in accordance with the definitions and discussions of each factor in the appropriate sections of the regulations, which will provide insight into the adjudicative weight to be accorded each factor.

201.00 Maximum sustained work capability limited to sedentary work as a result of severe medically determinable impairment(s).

(a)   Most sedentary occupations fall within the skilled, semi-skilled, professional, administrative, technical, clerical, and bench work classifications. Approximately 200 separate unskilled sedentary occupations can be identified, each representing numerous jobs in the national economy. Approximately 85 percent of these jobs are in the machine trades and bench work occupational categories. These jobs (unskilled sedentary occupations) may be performed after a short demonstration or within 30 days.

(b)   These unskilled sedentary occupations are standard within the industries in which they exist. While sedentary work represents a significantly restricted range of work, this range in itself is not so prohibitively restricted as to negate work capability for substantial gainful activity.

(c)   Vocational adjustment to sedentary work may be expected where the individual has special skills or experience relevant to sedentary work or where age and basic educational competencies provide sufficient occupational mobility to adapt to the major segment of unskilled sedentary work. Inability to engage in substantial gainful activity would be indicated where an individual who is restricted to sedentary work because of a severe medically determinable impairment lacks special skills or experience relevant to sedentary work, lacks educational qualifications relevant to most sedentary work (e.g., has a limited education or less) and the individual's age, though not necessarily advanced, is a factor which significantly limits vocational adaptability.

(d)   The adversity of functional restrictions to sedentary work at advanced age (55 and over) for individuals with no relevant past work or who can no longer perform vocationally relevant past work and have no transferable skills, warrants a finding of disabled in the absence of the rare situation where the individual has recently completed education which provides a basis for direct entry into skilled sedentary work. Advanced age and a history of unskilled work or no work experience would ordinarily offset any vocational advantages that might accrue by reason of any remote past education, whether it is more or less than limited education.

(e)   The presence of acquired skills that are readily transferable to a significant range of skilled work within an individual's residual functional capacity would ordinarily warrant a finding of ability to engage in substantial gainful activity regardless of the adversity of age, or whether the individual's formal education is commensurate with his or her demonstrated skill level. The acquisition of work skills demonstrates the ability to perform work at the level of complexity demonstrated by the skill level attained regardless of the individual's formal educational attainments.

(f)   In order to find transferability of skills to skilled sedentary work for individuals who are of advanced age (55 and over), there must be very little, if any, vocational adjustment required in terms of tools, work processes, work settings, or the industry.

(g)   Individuals approaching advanced age (age 50-54) may be significantly limited in vocational adaptability if they are restricted to sedentary work. When such individuals have no past work experience or can no longer perform vocationally relevant past work and have no transferable skills, a finding of disabled ordinarily obtains. However, recently completed education which provides for direct entry into sedentary work will preclude such a finding. For this age group, even a high school education or more (ordinarily completed in the remote past) would have little impact for effecting a vocational adjustment unless relevant work experience reflects use of such education.

(h)(1)   The term younger individual is used to denote an individual age 18 through 49. For individuals who are age 45-49, age is a less advantageous factor for making an adjustment to other work than for those who are age 18-44. Accordingly, a finding of "disabled" is warranted for individuals age 45-49 who:
(i)   Are restricted to sedentary work,
(ii)   Are unskilled or have no transferable skills,
(iii)   Have no past relevant work or can no longer perform past relevant work, and

(iv)   Are unable to communicate in English, or are able to speak and understand English but are unable to read or write in English.
(2)   For individuals who are under age 45, age is a more advantageous factor for making an adjustment to other work. It is usually not a significant factor in limiting such individuals' ability to make an adjustment to other work, including an adjustment to unskilled sedentary work, even when the individuals are unable to communicate in English or are illiterate in English.
(3)   Nevertheless, a decision of "disabled" may be appropriate for some individuals under age 45 (or individuals age 45-49 for whom rule 201.17 does not direct a decision of disabled) who do not have the ability to perform a full range of sedentary work. However, the inability to perform a full range of sedentary work does not necessarily equate with a finding of "disabled." Whether an individual will be able to make an adjustment to other work requires an adjudicative assessment of factors such as the

type and extent of the individual's limitations or restrictions and the extent of the erosion of the occupational base. It requires an individualized determination that considers the impact of the limitations or restrictions on the number of sedentary, unskilled occupations or the total number of jobs to which the individual may be able to adjust, considering his or her age, education and work experience, including any transferable skills or education providing for direct entry into skilled work.

(4)   "Sedentary work" represents a significantly restricted range of work, and individuals with a maximum sustained work capability limited to sedentary work have very serious functional limitations. Therefore, as with any case, a finding that an individual is limited to less than the full range of sedentary work will be based on careful consideration of the evidence of the individual's medical impairment(s) and the limitations and restrictions attributable to it. Such evidence must support the finding that the individual's residual functional capacity is limited to less than the full range of sedentary work.

(i)   While illiteracy or the inability to communicate in English may significantly limit an individual's vocational scope, the primary work functions in the bulk of unskilled work relate to working with things (rather than with data or people) and in these work functions at the unskilled level, literacy or ability to communicate in English has the least significance. Similarly the lack of relevant work experience would have little significance since the bulk of unskilled jobs require no qualifying work experience. Thus, the functional capability for a full range of sedentary work represents sufficient numbers of jobs to indicate substantial vocational scope for those individuals age 18-44 even if they are illiterate or unable to communicate in English.

202.00 Maximum sustained work capability limited to light work as a result of severe medically determinable impairment(s).

(a)   The functional capacity to perform a full range of light work includes the functional capacity to perform sedentary as well as light work. Approximately 1,600 separate sedentary and light unskilled occupations can be identified in eight broad occupational categories, each occupation representing numerous jobs in the national economy. These jobs can be performed after a short demonstration or within 30 days, and do not require special skills or experience.

(b)   The functional capacity to perform a wide or full range of light work represents substantial work capability compatible with making a work adjustment to substantial numbers of unskilled jobs and, thus, generally provides sufficient occupational mobility even for severely impaired individuals who are not of advanced age and have sufficient educational competencies for unskilled work.

(c)   However, for individuals of advanced age who can no longer perform vocationally relevant past work and who have a history of unskilled work experience, or who have only skills that are not readily transferable to a significant range of semi-skilled or skilled work that is within the individual's functional capacity, or who have no work experience, the limitations in vocational adaptability represented by functional restriction to light work warrant a finding of disabled. Ordinarily, even a high school education or more which was completed in the remote past will have little positive impact on effecting a vocational adjustment unless relevant work experience reflects use of such education.

(d)   Where the same factors in paragraph (c) of this section regarding education and work experience are present, but where age, though not advanced, is a factor which significantly limits vocational adaptability (i.e., closely approaching advanced age, 50-54) and an individual's vocational scope is further significantly limited by illiteracy or inability to communicate in English, a finding of disabled is warranted.

(e)   The presence of acquired skills that are readily transferable to a significant range of semi-skilled or skilled work within an individual's residual functional capacity would ordinarily warrant a finding of not disabled regardless of the adversity of age, or whether the individual's formal education is commensurate with his or her demonstrated skill level. The acquisition of work skills demonstrates the ability to perform work at the level of complexity demonstrated by the skill level attained regardless of the individual's formal educational attainments.

(f)   For a finding of transferability of skills to light work for individuals of advanced age who are closely approaching retirement age (age 60-64), there must be very little, if any, vocational adjustment required in terms of tools, work processes, work settings, or the industry.

(g)   While illiteracy or the inability to communicate in English may significantly limit an individual's vocational scope, the primary work functions in the bulk of unskilled work relate to working with things (rather than with data or people) and in these work functions at the unskilled level, literacy or ability to communicate in English has the least significance. Similarly, the lack of relevant work experience would have little significance since the bulk of unskilled jobs require no qualifying work experience. The capability for light work, which includes the ability to do sedentary work, represents the capability for substantial numbers of such jobs. This, in turn, represents substantial vocational scope for younger individuals (age 18-49) even if illiterate or unable to communicate in English.

203.00 Maximum sustained work capability limited to medium work as a result of severe medically determinable impairment(s).

(a)   The functional capacity to perform medium work includes the functional capacity to perform sedentary, light, and medium work. Approximately 2,500 separate sedentary, light, and medium occupations can be identified, each occupation representing numerous jobs in the national economy which do not require skills or previous experience and which can be performed after a short demonstration or within 30 days.

(b)   The functional capacity to perform medium work represents such substantial work capability at even the unskilled level that a finding of disabled is ordinarily not warranted in cases where a severely impaired individual retains the functional capacity to perform medium work. Even the adversity of advanced age (55 or over) and a work history of unskilled work may be offset by the substantial work capability represented by the functional capacity to perform medium work. However, we will find that an individual who (1) has a marginal education, (2) has work experience of 35 years or more during which he or she did only arduous unskilled physical labor, (3) is not working, and (4) is no longer able to do this kind of work because of a severe impairment(s) is disabled, even though the individual is able to do medium work. (See § 404.1562(a) in this subpart and § 416.962(a) in subpart I of part 416.)

(c)   However, the absence of any relevant work experience becomes a more significant adversity for individuals of advanced age (55 and over). Accordingly, this factor, in combination with a limited education or less, militates against making a vocational adjustment to even this substantial range of work and a finding of disabled is appropriate. Further, for individuals closely approaching retirement age (60-64) with a work history of unskilled work and with marginal education or less, a finding of disabled is appropriate.

www.ingramcontent.com/pod-product-compliance
Lightning Source LLC
Chambersburg PA
CBHW081423280526
45788CB00009B/3213